SOLID GROUND

SOLID GROUND

VICTOR BOOKS®

A DIVISION OF SCRIPTURE PRESS PUBLICATIONS INC.
USA CANADA ENGLAND

Portions of "The Pharisee and Me" quoted throughout the text are reprinted from *Heartbeat*, © 1990 by Jill Briscoe. Used by permission of Harold Shaw Publishers, Wheaton, Ill.

Most Scripture quotations are taken from the *Holy Bible, New International Version*, © 1973, 1978, 1984, International Bible Society. Used by permission of Zondervan Bible Publishers. Other quotations are from the *Authorized (King James) Version.*

Recommended Dewey Decimal Classification: 248.833
Suggested Subject Heading: PERSONAL CHRISTIANITY FOR WOMEN

ISBN: 0-89693-884-0

1 2 3 4 5 6 7 8 9 10 Printing/Year 96 95 94 93 92

VICTOR BOOKS
A division of SP Publications, Inc.
      Wheaton, Illinois 60187

•CONTENTS•

Recognition to Beth Donigan Seversen
for assistance
in researching and formulating
parts of this book.

• INTRODUCTION •

Jesus said we need to build our lives on the solid principles He taught us if we are to withstand the storms of life. Those principles are set out in the Sermon on the Mount. By putting His Word into action, we can know real happiness, for "blessed are those who are not only hearers of the Word but doers of it." That's what Jesus said.

• BEFORE YOU BEGIN •

People who gather together for Bible study are likely to be at different places in their spiritual lives, and their study materials should be flexible enough to meet their different needs. This book is designed to be used as a Bible study guide for such groups in homes or churches. It can also be used by individuals who are studying on their own. The lessons are written in five distinct sections, so that they can be used in a variety of situations. Groups and individuals alike can choose to use the elements they find most useful in the order they find most beneficial.

These studies will help you learn some new truths from the Bible as well as how to dig out those truths. You will learn not only *what* the Bible says, but how to use Scripture to deepen your relationship with Jesus Christ by obeying it and applying it in daily living. Potential leaders will learn how to lead a discussion in a nonthreatening setting.

What You'll Need
For each study you will need a Bible and this Bible study guide. You might also want to have a notebook in which to record your thoughts

and discoveries from your personal study and group meetings. A notebook could also be used to record prayer requests from the group.

The Sections

Food for Thought. This is a devotional narrative that introduces the topic, person, or passage featured in the lesson. There are several ways it can be used. Each person could read it before coming to the group meeting, and someone could briefly summarize it at the beginning. It could be read silently by each person at the beginning of the session, or it could be read aloud, by one or several group members. (Suggested time: 10 minutes)

Talking It Over. This section contains discussion questions to help you review what you learned in Food for Thought. There are also questions to help you apply the narrative's truths to daily life. The person who leads the discussion of these questions need not be a trained or experienced teacher. All that is needed is someone to keep things moving and facilitate group interaction. (Suggested time: 30 minutes)

Praying It Through. This is a list of suggestions for prayer based on the lesson. You may want to use all the suggestions or eliminate some in order to leave more time for personal sharing and prayer requests. (Suggested time: 20 minutes)

Digging Deeper. The questions in this section are also related to the passage, topic, or character from the lesson. But they will not always be limited to the exact passage or character from Food for Thought. Passages and characters from both the Old and New Testaments will appear in this section, in order to show how God has worked through *all* of history in people's lives. These questions will require a little more thinking and some digging into Scripture, as well as some use of Bible study tools. Participants will be stretched as they become experienced in the "how-tos" of Bible study. (Suggested time: 45 minutes)

Tool Chest. The Tool Chest contains a description of a specific type of Bible study help and includes an explanation of how it is used. An example of the tool is given, and an example of it or excerpt from it is usually included in the Digging Deeper study.

The Bible study helps in the Tool Chest can be purchased by anyone who desires to build a basic library of Bible study reference books and other tools. They would also be good additions to a church library. Some are reasonably inexpensive, but others are quite expensive. A few may be available in your local library or in a seminary or college library. A group might decide to purchase one tool during each series and build a corporate tool chest for all the members of the group to use. You can never be too young a Christian to begin to master Bible study helps, nor can you be too old to learn new methods of rightly dividing the Word of truth.

Options for Group Use

Different groups, made up of people at diverse stages of spiritual growth, will want to use the elements in this book in different ways. Here are a few suggestions to get you started, but be creative and sensitive to your group's needs.

☐ Spend 5-15 minutes at the beginning of the group time introducing yourselves and having group members answer an icebreaker question. (Sample icebreaker questions are included under Tips for Leaders.)

☐ Extend the prayer time to include sharing of prayer requests, praise items, or things group members have learned recently in their times of personal Bible study.

☐ The leader could choose questions for discussion from the Digging Deeper section based on whether participants have prepared ahead of time or not.

☐ The entire group could break into smaller groups to allow different groups to use different sections. (The smaller groups could move to other rooms in the home or church where you are meeting.)

Tips for Leaders

Preparation

1. Pray for the Holy Spirit's guidance as you study, that you will be equipped to teach the lesson and make it appealing and applicable.

2. Read through the entire lesson and any Bible passages or verses that are mentioned. Answer all the questions.

3. Become familiar enough with the lesson that, if time in the group is running out, you know which questions could most easily be left out.

4. Gather all the items you will need for the study: name tags, extra pens, extra Bibles.

The Meeting

1. Start and end on time.

2. Have everyone wear a name tag until group members know one another's names.

3. Have each person introduce himself or herself, or ask regular

attenders to introduce guests.

4. For each meeting, pick an icebreaker question or another activity to help group members get to know one another better.

5. Use any good ideas to make everyone feel comfortable.

The Discussion

1. Ask the questions, but try to let the group answer. Don't be afraid of silence. Reword the question if it is unclear to the group or answer it yourself to clarify.

2. Encourage everyone to participate. If someone is shy, ask that person to answer a nonthreatening question or give an opinion. If someone tends to monopolize the discussion, thank that person for his or her contribution and ask if someone else has anything he or she would like to add. (Or ask that person to make the coffee!)

3. If someone gives an incorrect answer, don't bluntly or tactlessly tell him or her so. If it is partly right, reinforce that. Ask if anyone else has any thoughts on the subject. (Disagree agreeably!)

4. Avoid tangents. If someone is getting off the subject, ask that person how his or her point relates to the lesson.

5. Don't feel threatened if someone asks a question you can't answer. Tell the person you don't know but will find out before the next meeting—then be sure to find out! Or ask if someone would like to research and present the answer at the group's next meeting.

Icebreaker Questions

The purpose of these icebreaker questions is to help the people in your group get to know one another over the course of the study. The questions you use when your group members don't know one another very well should be very general and nonthreatening. As time goes on, your questions can become more focused and specific. Always give group members the option of passing if they think a question is too personal.

What do you like to do for fun?
What is your favorite season? dessert? book?
What would be your ideal vacation?
What exciting thing happened to you this week?
What was the most memorable thing you did with your family when you were a child?
What one word best describes the way you feel today?
Tell three things you are thankful for.
Imagine that your house is on fire. What three things would you

try to take with you on your way out?
If you were granted one wish, what would it be?
What experience of your past would you most enjoy reliving?
What quality do you most appreciate in a friend?
What is your pet peeve?
What is something you are learning to do or trying to get better at?
What is your greatest hope?
What is your greatest fear?
What one thing would you like to change about yourself?
What has been the greatest accomplishment of your life?
What has been the greatest disappointment of your life?

Need More Help?

Here is a list of books that contain helpful information on leading discussions and working in groups:

> *How to Lead Small Group Bible Studies* (NavPress, 1982).
> *Creative Bible Learning for Adults,* Monroe Marlowe and Bobbie Reed (Regal, 1977).
> *Getting Together,* Em Griffin (InterVarsity Press, 1982).
> *Good Things Come in Small Groups* (InterVarsity Press, 1985).

One Last Thought

This book is a tool you can use whether you have one or one hundred people who want to study the Bible and whether you have one or no teachers. Don't wait for a brilliant Bible study leader to appear—most such teachers acquired their skills by starting with a book like this and learning as they went along. Torrey said, "The best way to begin, is to begin." Happy beginnings!

1

Blessed Are the Poor in Spirit

•FOOD FOR THOUGHT•

Solid ground: that's what people are looking for. They want something firm beneath their feet, a sense of security, a safe place to stand. Jesus said if we hear His words and obey them, our lives will have that solid certainty about them.

The Sermon on the Mount recorded in Matthew is the first of five discourses by Jesus. It begins with the Beatitudes, and it finishes with a little parable about a wise and foolish man (Matt. 7:24-29). Jesus said the wise man builds his life on good foundations. It doesn't really matter how grand the house is above the ground—how colorful or even how expensive it appears—what really matters is the part that is out of sight. What is the house built upon? If we build our lives wisely, we will find our houses standing firm when the storms come. If we build foolishly, we will be swept away.

All our dreams may well be turned into nightmares in the face of a personal calamity. Who hasn't experienced a life overwhelmed with a storm of sorrow, or lashed by the pitiless rain of rejection? Some people collapse—blown over by the winds of change in a cruel world, while others withstand—with grand fortitude—a breakdown of their marriage, financial misfortune, the trauma of a pregnant teenager, or medical misery in their last days—by standing firm on Christ.

When the Lord gave this wonderful talk, His disciples listened attentively. So did the Pharisees and all the people that were gathered on that occasion. Jesus hoped His disciples would build lives that would be firmly anchored on Him. He also knew the Pharisees that were listening might pay lip service to God, but their hearts were far from Him. All the people listening to Jesus had a choice; so do we!

13

Those of us who profess to be Christians have a disciple within us, but we also have a Pharisee. The Pharisee is a picture of the old nature. I remember the day I discovered a Pharisee in me! It was quite a shock.

> "One day I found within my heart
> someone who'd been there from the start.
> A prudish person — self-appointed,
> self-sufficient — self-annointed.
> Though I a true disciple be,
> I've met the Pharisee in me!"

Every day the believer has to settle an eternal dispute that rages within the heart. Will we be wise people, disciples, or will we be Pharisees? In other words, will we live after the spirit or after the flesh? Will we be self-made men or Christ-made ones? The answer to that question will determine whether our lives will crash around our ears.

If we would be wise, we will use the eight attitudes in Matthew 5 as foundational building blocks on which to erect the structure of our daily lives. The first building block is humility. "Blessed are the poor in spirit," said Jesus! (Matt. 5:3) Happy is the one who develops an attitude of sweet humility. But just what is humility?

Spiritually prosperous people are humble. They feel themselves destitute in the realm of the spirit. Being humble doesn't mean we should be poor spirited, but rather, we should have a huge sense of how poor and needy we really are. When we acknowledge our spiritual bankruptcy before God, we find ourselves, of necessity, developing a dependency on Him instead of being independent. As the disciple grows, so will his sense of spiritual poverty. The Pharisee in me, however, will deny his need, trusting rather in his own self-sufficiency. So what are some practical ways we can build such saving humility into our lives?

First, we must acknowledge our need for such an attitude. Those convinced of their spiritual poverty recognize they are poor in the sense that they can do no good thing without divine assistance. In other words, we have to admit we are not strong enough, knowledgeable enough, clever enough, or spiritual enough to be disciples of Jesus Christ! We simply don't have what it takes. So if we realize we need divine assistance we'll want the Divine One to assist us as we build our house. How can He assist us?

We will need a good system of Bible reading. As we read the Word of God, we will come across Jesus' instructions. Some of those words will be orders, rules, and commands. We should underline them, think about them, and above all do them. This will require strength from God. Disciples will, therefore, develop their prayer lives. The Pharisee in us will not! Those that are poor in spirit are much in prayer, ever begging for heavenly alms. The Pharisee stands in God's presence with unbowed head and prays, "I thank You, God, that I am not as other men. I do this and I do that and I do the other—all for You. In fact, I do all this without having to bother You at all!"

Through reading and acting on the Word of God and using prayer to speak to Him of our need for His power and assistance, we will find ourselves in lots of situations that will cause us to practice dependence. This in turn will produce humility.

Humility is a sign of spiritual maturity. The Bible is like a looking glass, and humility helps us to look in this moral mirror and see ourselves as we really are. If we are honest, we can recognize our spiritual blemishes and choose to do something about them.

When our little grandson Andrew was very small, he used to love to look at himself in the mirror. He was fascinated by the baby that looked back at him. My daughter told me her baby books said he didn't know it was himself he was seeing. That came later when he had matured a little.

How like some of us, I reflected. We look into the Bible and instead of seeing our own reflection, we see *another baby* instead. "This verse describes Aunt Mabel exactly," we say! Maturity brings personal recognition as we gaze into the wonderful law of liberty.

It shouldn't be so hard! After all, we entered the kingdom with humility. As the hymn, "Rock of Ages," reminds us . . .

> "Nothing in my hand I bring,
> Simply to Thy cross I cling;
> Naked, come to Thee for dress,
> Helpless, look to Thee for grace;
> Foul, I to the fountain fly,
> Wash me, Savior, or I die!"

So as Paul said, "As ye have therefore received Christ Jesus the Lord, so walk ye in Him" (Col. 2:6, KJV). We need to continue as we began, and follow in His steps.

It helps not to take oneself too seriously. To laugh often and hard at ourselves is medicine for the soul—and a scourge of pride. The Pharisee in me won't be able to do that. He never laughs about anything. He thinks more highly of himself than he ought to think, and he never sees himself as really rather ridiculous. It also helps to have kids, teenagers in particular, or some close and honest friend who will surely cut us down to size when we need it!

Getting out of our comfort zone helps as well. Try volunteering for a task you have never attempted before—something that will put you at risk and therefore ensure you depend on Him. Stretching our abilities means we will fail on the way to succeeding. It's a humbling thing to fail, and yet, a healthy thing to learn to handle it with good humor and humility.

If we build on Him as our life's foundation, we'll be all right when the storms come. We won't, like the Pharisee, try to batten down the hatches and wait it out all on our own. A poverty of spirit is repugnant to the Pharisee; such a poverty is so opposed to his fancied excellence. The Pharisee will never count Christ precious, but rather he will rely on his own religious resources and efforts to pull him through.

That sort of approach won't work of course. Great will be the fall of the life that builds on the shifting sand of self-sufficiency. We must deal with the Pharisee in us. We should ignore his protests and turn a deaf ear to his cries. We must follow Jesus' example and learn of Him, for He is meek and lowly in heart, and we shall find rest for our souls. "Blessed are the poor in spirit," said Jesus, "for theirs is the kingdom of heaven" (Matt. 5:3).

•TALKING IT OVER•

Suggested Times

---

1. Read Matthew 5:3.
   ☐ Recap and discuss what it means to be poor in spirit.
   ☐ Do you think this concept appears to conflict with some "self-concept" of the present day?

10 minutes

---

2. Read Matthew 7:1-5.
   ☐ Discuss the fight in the human heart between the disciple and the Pharisee. How do the disciple and the Pharisee present a picture of the Spirit and the flesh?
   ☐ Read Romans 7:14-25.
   Which verse speaks to you and why?
   ☐ Give a personal example of the battle between the disciple and the Pharisee in you.

20 minutes

---

3. Read Matthew 18:1-3.
   Why do you think Jesus chose a child to model humility?

5 minutes

17

•PRAYING IT THROUGH•

*Suggested
Times*

1. ☐ Praise God for who He is.   *5 minutes*
   ☐ Admit to God what you are not.
   ☐ Thank God for making you dependent on Him
   and for His power that helps you stand on solid
   ground.

2. ☐ Pray for people you know who are building their   *10 minutes*
   lives on shifting sand.
   ☐ Pray for people whose lives are built on the
   Rock, but who are weathering a storm.
   ☐ Pray for yourself—that you will have your feet
   on solid ground at all times.

3. Take a few moments to meditate on Matthew 5   *5 minutes*
   and see your own reflection in the perfect law of
   liberty.

•DIGGING DEEPER•

1. Read Matthew 5–7 in one sitting and outline these three chapters by creating a simple title for each new paragraph or new topic introduced. The first one is done for you.

Reference	Title	Major Theme
5:1-11	Attitude consistent with the kingdom of heaven	Kingdom character traits

Group these titles under major categories or themes.

2. What key words are repeated in these chapters? What is their significance?

3. What major themes did you discover in your reading? (cf. Matt. 5:3, 10, 12, 19-20; 6:10, 33; 7:14, 21)

4. Describe the setting. Who was present? What was the occasion? (cf. Matt. 4:23–5:2; 7:28-29)

5. Are there any patterns of ascending or descending degrees among the Beatitudes in verses 5:3-10?

6. Which reward or blessing is repeated? To start and finish with the same phrase is a technique the Greeks employed called *inclusion*. It conveys that a thought has been completed and that all the material contained within is related to a particular subject. Looking at what is repeated in this inclusion, what is most likely the subject of the Beatitudes?

7. How does each condition in the Beatitudes relate to its corresponding blessing? Rewrite the Beatitudes in your own words. The first one is done for you.

   Matthew 5:3–If you recognize your spiritual poverty before God, you will be accepted into His heaven.

   5:4

   5:5

   5:6

   5:7

   5:8

   5:9

   5:10

8. Look up the word *poor* in *Webster's New Collegiate Dictionary* (1981).

Below, write out definitions 4a and 4b.

9. With what is the word *poor* associated in these Scriptures?

   Psalm 34:6

   Isaiah 57:15

   Isaiah 66:1-2

   Luke 4:18

10. To be *poor in spirit* is to acknowledge your impoverished spiritual condition before God and to repent of your spiritual bankruptcy. It is to admit that God is everything, that you are nothing, and that you lack the necessary resources to be accepted by Him. It is to confess your need for God and ask for His mercy, forgiveness, and acceptance. Have you met this condition for receiving the kingdom of heaven? Write a prayer of your own detailed response to this question in the space provided.

11. In spending time with tax collectors and sinners (Matt. 9:11), the Lord Jesus gives us excellent object lessons for the spiritual conditions required to be a recipient of the kingdom of heaven. Think of specific examples of people to whom Christ Jesus offered the kingdom of heaven. Describe their physical and spiritual status.

12. Spend time in prayer praising God for the gift of eternal life, confessing your need for Him, thanking Him for accepting you in

Christ, and interceding for loved ones who have not yet met the spiritual requirement of being "poor in spirit" needed for entrance into the kingdom of heaven.

For Further Study
1. Read Donald A. Carson's discussion of the kingdom of heaven in *The Sermon on the Mount, An Evangelical Exposition of Matthew 5–7* (Baker Book House, 1978, pp. 11-15).
2. Do a word study of the Bible's use of the words *humble* and *humility*.
3. Memorize Matthew 5:3.

•TOOL CHEST•
(A Suggested Optional Resource)

THE SERMON ON THE MOUNT
AN EVANGELICAL EXPOSITION OF MATTHEW 5-7
Dr. Donald Carson teaches New Testament at Trinity Evangelical Divinity School, Deerfield, Illinois. He has a rare and tremendous spiritual gift, combining excellent scholarship with a pastoral heart. He first prepared this exposition on the Sermon on the Mount for university students in England, speaking to hundreds who came together on Saturday evenings to learn from the Scriptures. Using language the lay person can comprehend, he masterfully unveils the Sermon on the Mount, its meanings, and how it should practically impact everyday life. This resource will both challenge and bless you. It is available in paperback from Baker Book House.

2
Blessed Are Those Who Mourn

•FOOD FOR THOUGHT•

"Blessed are those who mourn," said Jesus, "for they will be comforted" (Matt. 5:4). The word *pentheo*, to mourn, is a pretty miserable one! It speaks of tears, inconsolable grief, guilt, and depression. And yet, this mourning is not to be for a lost loved one, but rather for the poverty-stricken spiritual state of our souls. It speaks of our inability to shape up to God's expectations. The Lord said, "Happy are the completely penitent."

John Stott in his book, *Christian Counter Culture*, says, "One might almost translate this second beatitude 'Happy are the unhappy' in order to draw attention to the startling paradox it contains. What kind of sorrow can it be which brings the joy of Christ's blessing to those who feel it? It is plain from the context that those here promised comfort are not primarily those who mourn the loss of a loved one, but those who mourn the loss of their innocence, their righteousness, their self-respect. It is not the sorrow of bereavement to which Christ refers, but the sorrow of repentance. This is the second stage of spiritual blessing. It is one thing to be spiritually poor and acknowledge it; it is another to grieve and to mourn over it. Or, in more theological language, confession is one thing, contrition is another."[1]

You may ask, "But how could such a miserable feeling make me happy?" The answer to your question is that mourning is the way to comfort, consolation, forgiveness, affirmation, and divine affirmation. It sounds upside down—but then the Christian life is a paradox. We give to get, we die to live, we mourn to dance!

---

[1]John R.W. Stott, *Christian Counter-Culture* (IVP, 1978), pp. 40-41.

To find out what the word *pentheo* actually means, we have to see where else it is used in Scripture. In Matthew 9:15 it describes the mourning of a bridegroom snatched from his bride. Can you imagine being on the way to your wedding, having a car crash, and seeing your fiancé die? What would you feel like?

In Matthew 16:9-10 *pentheo* is used to describe the group of mourning disciples after the crucifixion. What must it have been like to see your Master, leader, and friend—for whom you had left home and family—being so terribly mutilated, tortured, and killed? How would you feel about that?

Pentheo is also used to describe the total involvement of the whole personality as in the case of a distraught crying child. This total misery found its expression in Ishmael's cry when he was near death. "Then she [Hagar] went off and sat down nearby, about a bowshot away, for she thought, 'I cannot watch the boy die' "(Gen. 21:16). *Pentheo* is also used to describe the loud lamentation of mothers wailing for their slaughtered children (Jer. 31:15). Shut your eyes and try to feel such intense grief, a grief that can hardly be assuaged.

In Old Testament times, there were certain customs when people mourned. A period of seven days was set aside. There would be a beating of breasts and shaving of beards. Dirges were sung, sackcloth was worn, and people loudly wailed. They were, as you can see, extremely serious about the act of mourning.

Now let me ask you—as I have asked myself—do you take sin as seriously as this? Your sin? Do you mourn your sinfulness to such a degree? If so, you will be strangely comforted for the Holy Spirit delights to encourage the person who so mourns his or her spiritual impoverishment!

I hazard a guess that most of us are rather like my oldest grandchild who, when told "No, Danny" by my husband Stuart for the umpteenth time, replied sweetly, "Papa Stu—I don't know what 'no' is!" Do we, like Danny, say, "Papa God, I don't know what *no* is," instead of working hard on developing this happy, contrite nature?

So how then do we go about becoming people who are truly sorry when we sin? First, we have to be honest with ourselves. If we are not truly sorry, then we can start by at least being sorry that we are not! That's something we can all do! We can grieve our haughty hearts and dare to ask God to bring conviction.

Second, we have to be brave. Maybe you are thinking to yourself, "I don't like all this talk about having a broken spirit. Perhaps life has broken me already and I don't need more brokenness." Perhaps we have been broken by other people's sins—the neglect of an alcoholic father or the sexual abuse of a relative; the unfaithfulness of a spouse or a health problem. Maybe we have sinned ourselves and try to pretend it didn't happen. Then again, we may make excuses for our behavior or lay blame on others. But to mourn our sinfulness in the correct sense leads to healing and relief and a useful flourishing life. Remember, God promises He will give us gladness for mourning, a spirit of praise instead of a sense of despair, and a fruitful, useful life (Isa. 61:3-5).

This spirit is, of course, anathema to the Pharisee in me. While God wants us to be a publican in attitude, the Pharisee in me fights the very idea. While the publican in the Bible prays, "O Lord, I am so sorry I am who I am. Be merciful to me, a sinner," the Pharisee is praising himself for being righteous (in his own eyes). He is hoping too that his clever erudite prayer is being overheard and applauded by passersby. Do you recognize the Pharisee?

> "Oh, Lord, I pray hard on my way
> I try to do it every day
> a publican to be, I try
> and beat my breast and sigh and cry
> I'm hoping others round will see —
> oops — there's the Pharisee in me!"

For Christians there is a daily choice: to keep our hearts right with God. Then when our hearts are comforted by the Lord, He expects another sort of mourning — this time for other people's sins!

So we will need to be honest, brave, and then inclusive! Stott says,"Jesus wept over the sins of others, over their bitter consequences in judgment and death, and over the impenitent city which would not receive Him. We too should weep more over the evil in the world, as did the godly men of biblical times. 'My eyes shed streams of tears,' the psalmist could say to God, 'because men do not keep Thy law' "[2] (Ps. 119:136).

We should mourn for others because people around us do not mourn for themselves. Men and women live as enemies of Christ, listening to false teachers, and falling into sexual sin and debauchery (Phil. 3:18 and 2 Cor. 12:21). A true sense of our own and other people's sin will make great intercessors out of us! (Read Daniel, Chapter 9.)

So how, practically, do I go about this *happy mourning?* First, I need

---

[2]Ibid., p. 41.

to be specific. At the end of the day I need to go to God through Christ my great High Priest and go over my day step by step. I need to name particularly the sins of omission and sins of commission. I must remember the wrong that I have done and realize the right things I haven't gotten around to doing. I will need to ask His forgiveness and then believe He has cleansed me (1 John 1:9).

What will be the result of such an ongoing attitude? Revival! There will be new life and blessing not only in my own life but in the lives of others.

The Word gives us an authority for our faith, but it also makes us face ourselves before the refining eyes of God's holiness. We see ourselves in the light of Jesus Christ. In His sight our righteousness is as filthy rags (Isaiah 64:6). The props of self-sufficiency are knocked out from under our pride. We are found out for what we are—sinners.

As the dreadful sense of guilt increases, the awful realization of impending judgment deepens. A holy fear grips our hearts, and we may be left with the feeling of utter helplessness. There is no place to hide from God. One thing is certain: when the Spirit truly convicts our souls, however it may be felt, sin cannot be treated with indifference. Frivolity and lightheartedness are gone. We do not have to be urged to flee from the wrath to come. When we are broken and contrite in spirit, our hearts are disposed to heed any offer of mercy. In time of complacency it may be necessary to get men to come to Christ, but in the throes of revival "sinners beg Christ to receive them."

Once we have been awakened to our need, we must do something about it. Conviction of sin leads to repentance. There can be no revival until we confess our sin, turn from our evil ways, and throw ourselves upon God's mercy. "If I regard iniquity in my heart, the Lord will not hear me" (Psalm 66:18).

Any impediment to the flow of God's grace must be removed: unbelief, lust, lying, cheating, unclean thoughts, filthy speech, dirty habits, cursing, ingratitude, indifference to responsibility, disregard of self-discipline, prayerlessness, robbing God of tithes, Sabbath breaking, neglect of the poor, racial discrimination, an unforgiving spirit, backbiting, envy, jealousy, bitterness, deceitfulness, selfishness, hypocrisy. Whatever it is, whether a deed or a disposition, if known to be contrary to the holiness of God, it must be confessed and forsaken.

There can be no compromise. Repentance is a thorough housecleaning. Not only must confession be made to God; we must do all we can to make things right with people we have wronged. If we try to trim the corners and excuse a few favorite shortcomings, we are fooling ourselves. No revival can come in our hearts until sin is out of the way. Furthermore, until this is true of our own lives, we stand in the way of God's blessing to others.[3]

We can bring revival to our neighborhood, town, and our world. So God can use a small vessel like you and me. But He cannot, nor will not, use a dirty one. May we learn what it is to have a humble, contrite spirit. This way when the storms come, our houses will stand firm based on the free forgiveness of God!

[3]Ronald Coleman, *The Spark That Ignites* (Worldwide, 1989), pp. 38-39.

• TALKING IT OVER •

1. (Group discussion)   *5 minutes*
   □ Discuss and recap what it means to mourn.
   □ How does the word *pentheo* help you to under-
     stand the experience of spiritual mourning?

2. How do we mourn?   *10 minutes*
   Discuss which of these conditions is hardest for
   you to fulfill and explain why.
   □ Be honest.
   □ Be brave.
   □ Be inclusive.
   □ Be specific.

3. Read 1 John 1:5-10.   *5 minutes*
   Discuss: How do these verses apply to the process
   of mourning?

4. What are the results of mourning?   *10 minutes*
   Read this account of revival in Nehemiah 8:1-9 and
   discuss. Then read Nehemiah 9–12. How were the
   people affected? (See Ezra 10.)

•PRAYING IT THROUGH•

*Suggested
Times*

1. Pray to God about your own heart response to this message.

5 minutes

2. Pray for your loved ones.

5 minutes

3. ☐ Pray for your church.
   ☐ Pray for your city.
   ☐ Pray for your world.

10 minutes

30

•DIGGING DEEPER•

1. Review chapter 1 and what it means to be *poor in spirit.*

2. What is being mourned in Matthew 5:4? Is your answer appropriate for this context?

3. Study the following examples of God's people mourning personal and corporate sin.

    Nehemiah 1:6-7

    Psalm 51

    Isaiah 6:5

    Romans 7:14-24

    Ezra 10:1-16

    Psalm 119:136

    Luke 19:41-44

    1 Corinthians 5:1-5

    2 Corinthians 12:21

Philippians 3:18

4. What do these people share in common? In each case, what is specifically causing their distress?

5. Notice the intensity of emotional anguish in the above references. How does the intensity of your own grief over personal, corporate, and national sin compare?

6. Describe genuine contrition. You might look it up in a dictionary. What are the components of contrition? How is it different from confession?

7. Does Matthew 5:4 refer to the bereavement of a loved one? What frequent mistake do some people make when interpreting this verse?

8. What comfort is available to us when we are truly contrite? What is our ultimate hope and what ought to be our eternal perspective?

Isaiah 40:1-5

Isaiah 61:1-3

Mark 10:45

1 John 1:9

Revelation 21:4

9. Have you offered to God today the sacrifices He desires? (See Ps. 51:17.) If not, take time to do so now and record your prayer of contrition.

For Further Study
1. Do a study of the Old Testament connection between consolation and the Messiah.
2. Memorize Matthew 5:4.

•TOOL CHEST•
(A Suggested Optional Resource)

THE MESSAGE OF THE SERMON ON THE MOUNT
In *The Message of the Sermon on the Mount* (IVP), John Stott unearths the profound and precious treasures of the Sermon on the Mount. He teaches how these truths can be abided by today in the face of a secular society. Stott helps the Bible student discover how such radical principles must be and can be lived out by the proponents of the Christian counterculture in the midst of our non-Christian world. In his usual manner, Stott eloquently and practically shows how Christ might address these principles to our contemporary setting.

3

Blessed Are the Meek

•FOOD FOR THOUGHT•

"Blessed are the meek," says Jesus (Matt. 5:5).

"Well, now," the unbeliever might say, "that sounds too much like being a church mouse! I knew I'd never smile again if I became a Christian!" But meek certainly doesn't mean weak and mousy. Unfortunately, some of us, even in the church, have been brought up reciting the children's prayer:

> "Gentle Jesus meek and mild,
> Look upon a little child.
> Pity my simplicity,
> Suffer me to come to thee..."

This concept has led a few to be quite convinced that Jesus is as weak and simple as a little child, too insipid to merit attention or allegiance. How very, very different from the truth!

The word *praus* (meek) has the sense of harnessed energy—or controlled strength. We are not talking about self-control, but rather Christ control. It doesn't mean cringing before God like a whipped and whimpering puppy, but letting the Lord take the reigns of our lives and harness us. Then we will be led to say what He wants us to say and do what He wants us to do.

Jesus demonstrated a gentle, quiet strength. He always showed forbearance and patient courtesy. What a stark contrast to the attitudes of our society which is always telling us, "Get ahead by intimidation; look out for number one." Billy Graham quotes a woman who said, "I want to climb the ladder of success, and I don't care whose

35

fingers I step on as I climb up the rungs!"[1]

This attitude of *meekness* is also quite foreign to the "Pharisee in me..."

> "He's there as I start out my week
> advising me that meek is weak.
> He's up before me every day,
> to figure out a better way
> than following Him submissively.
> I've met the Pharisee in me!"

So let's think about the two words that describe what meekness is all about: control and courtesy. First then, control—Christ control. This must be built into the very foundation of our life. But how?

The idea of being harnessed gives us a clue. The self nature is like a wild horse that must be tamed or broken in. It needs to be corralled. I think about the little donkey that Jesus rode into Jerusalem when He made His triumphant entry. The foal had never been ridden before. He was unbroken—yet he submitted to being harnessed by Christ and finished up carrying Him willingly where He wanted to go.

The Pharisee in me or my self nature says, "No Christ is going to sit on my back," or to be more colloquial, we say, "Get off my back, Jesus." The Pharisee in me doesn't want to be either fed or led by Jesus. But the disciple must be both fed and led if Christ is to be *lifted up* in his or her life. Just as the little donkey elevated Jesus Christ, a disciple of Christ submits to Him and willingly takes Him where He wants to go.

Jesus said, "Come to Me, all you who are weary and burdened, and I will give you rest. Take My yoke upon you and learn from Me, for I am gentle and humble in heart, and you will find rest for your souls" (Matt. 11:28-29). Jesus offers to harness our energies, load us up with cargo He wants us to carry, and lead us along the path He chooses for us. He promises us that this burden He asks us to bear for Him will be easy and light. To live a life sharing Christ's burdens will require a meek spirit. That takes Christian character.

The Pharisee in me, on the other hand, loves to load others up with burdens too heavy to bear. He carries little or nothing himself but contents himself with burdening those beneath him with so many heavy rules of religion that they collapse under the weight of them. When I catch the "old man" doing such things, I need to reject such behavior.

---

[1]Billy Graham, *The Secret of Happiness* (Grason, 1955), p. 65.

So how do I build my life on this foundational attitude of meekness?

First, I must evaluate areas of my life which have not been *broken in.* What wild part of me needs taming? What stubborn attitude is kicking up its heels in my life—trying to avoid God's control at any price? Second, I will need to meditate on the Scriptures. It will help me to look in the Bible for examples of wild people that God tamed and try with God's help to emulate them. A good example is Jacob, whose story is found in Genesis.

Ishmael also comes to mind—not least because he is described as a *wild donkey of a man.* In other words, he was always looking for a *fight.* Maybe you are like that! Then there was Moses. He is described as being the *meekest man in all the earth,* but in Numbers 11:10-15 we read that he gets sick of being meek! He loses his temper, throws the two tablets of stone out of his hands, and breaks the Ten Commandments. (Whenever we lose our tempers, we break the Ten Commandments too!) Moses had to go up the mountain again and recover his attitude. I've observed that meekness grows on the top of the mountain. I've climbed that particular mountain many times.

Then there was Paul. He is introduced to us on the road to Damascus. Jesus says to him, " 'Saul, Saul, why persecutest thou Me?' And he said, 'Who art Thou, Lord?' And the Lord said, 'I am Jesus whom thou persecutest: it is hard for thee to kick against the pricks' " (Acts 9:4-5, KJV). Paul sounds a little like a donkey to me! I hardly think the word meek would be the first word you would use to describe him. Yet Paul himself penned Galatians 5:22-23: "But the fruit of the Spirit is love, joy, peace, *patience*, kindness, goodness, faithfulness, gentleness, and *self-control.* Against such things there is no law" (italics added).

So Christ must be given permission to put bit and bridle on the wild donkey inside of us and bring us into line with His plans and purposes. The disciple in me will gladly hand over the reigns to Him. Once this is done, positive actions will result. My attitude will begin to show in loving respect and courtesy to others.

Billy Graham said, "We have glamorized vice and minimized virtue. We have played down gentleness, manners, and morals—while we have played up rudeness, savagery, and vice. We have reverted to the barbaric era of 'tooth and claw,' 'the survival of the fittest,' and the philosophy of 'might is right.' We are rich in knowledge but poor in wisdom; rich in the know-how of war but sadly lacking in gentleness, meekness, and faith. Individually, we are mechanisms of resentment, irritation, bitterness, and frustration!"[2]

---

[2]Ibid.

I remember coming to the U.S. from England and being appalled at the behavior in the church parking lot! I took an opportunity to tell the congregation I had observed a knock-down, drag-out, word fight over the parking place nearest to the church entrance. "What we need," I told our people earnestly, "is an awful lot more loving in the parking lot!" This generated a laugh, but the people knew exactly what I meant.

Jesus always had good manners. They were demonstrated in His treatment of women. He always treated the poor and the underprivileged with great dignity. He also expected others to do the same. He looked for ten (not one) cleansed lepers to return after their healing to say, "thank you," and He asked Simon—into whose house He had been invited—why a common courtesy of the day had not been extended to Him.

Good manners should begin at home. These graces are most often caught, not taught, and children will model after parents whose respect for each other is evident. Courtesy should be shown in the car when we drive and in the workplace where we work. Love has good manners. Love does not behave itself in an unseemly way, and love has respect for others' feelings. For this reason meek people will learn to let Christ harness their tongue and not allow it to gallop away on its own.

In our day there is a huge demand for honesty. We are encouraged to tell others what we feel. No matter what happens to the recipient, it will make us feel better and therefore must be done. But shouldn't we want the other person to feel better? To be brutally honest can amount to being brutally destructive. Consideration for the others' feelings should put a *rein* on our words.

A funny and true example will illustrate what I mean. Years ago someone sent me a newspaper cutting. The paper had been criticized for not reporting honestly enough, so they let it be known that for one issue only everything they wrote would be the whole brutal truth! Needless to say the issue sold out. Here is one excerpt:

> The Wednesday Literary Club met at the home of Mrs. So & So. The programme stated they were to study Shakespeare's play *Much Ado About Nothing*—they didn't! The lady who was asked to read the paper had never read the play and so they had no programme. But they made up for it by gossiping about everybody that wasn't there, and the whole afternoon was like the play, *much ado about nothing!*

Sometimes it's a kindly thing to do to withhold the truth! As we think of the word meek and realize the meaning, I hope we can let the meek Christ control us. The result will be a courteous, gentle attitude, compliant and sensitive to others.

"The Pharisee in me screams in derision at such ideas." Oh, he may make meek noises but he doesn't really mean them. He may pray in church, "God be merciful to me—a miserable sinner," but let anyone agree with that statement and he's likely to be terribly offended! However, if I would a true disciple be, I won't "think more highly of myself than I ought to think." I will, however, certainly "esteem others better than myself," and as John Stott says in *Christian Counter Culture*, "I myself am quite happy to recite the General Confession in church and call myself a 'miserable sinner.' It causes me no great problem. I can take it in my stride. But let somebody else come up to me after church and call me a miserable sinner, and I want to punch him on the nose! In other words, I am not prepared to allow other people to think or speak of me what I have just acknowledged before God that I am. There is a basic hypocrisy here; there always is when meekness is absent."

Blessed are the meek for they shall inherit the earth. Try it. You'll like it and so will others around you!

•TALKING IT OVER•

*Suggested
Times*

---

1. As a group, define and discuss the word meekness.   *4 minutes*

---

2. Read Genesis 21:8-20.   *10 minutes*
   □ Why was Ishmael mad at his little brother?
   □ What happened because he was uncontrolled?
   (Gen. 25:9)
   □ Do you think he got his own back whenever he
   had a chance? Do you blame him?
   □ What can we learn from this?

---

3. Read Numbers 12:1-16.   *10 minutes*
   □ Did Moses defend himself?
   □ Would God write a verse like verse 3 about you?
   □ What do you learn from this?

---

4. In small groups of two or three, review the ways to   *6 minutes*
   grow meekness and gentleness in our lives.
   □ Where *can* you begin?
   □ Where *will* you begin? Write a sentence to the
   Lord about your decision.

•PRAYING IT THROUGH•

Suggested Times

---

1. (On your own)
   - ☐ Read and meditate on 1 Corinthians 13. Remember that meekness is part of the fruit of love.
   - ☐ Pray quietly for all these aspects of true love to appear in your life.

   5 minutes

---

2. (Corporately)
   - ☐ Pray for people who profess Christ and who are untamed and doing a lot of damage in your . . .
     community
     city
     country
     world
   - ☐ Pray that Christ will tame the wild donkey in them.

   10 minutes

---

3. Pray for yourself that the sweet courtesy of Christ will be a strong attitude . . .
   - ☐ of yours
   - ☐ of your church leaders
   - ☐ of missionaries

   5 minutes

41

•DIGGING DEEPER•

1. Make a list of synonyms and antonyms for the word meek. After you have done so on your own, consult a reference tool such as a Greek-English lexicon of the New Testament by Bauer, Arndt, and Gingrich, and a Bible dictionary or commentary to complete your lists.

Synonyms	Antonyms

2. Look up *meek* in a concordance. What Bible character(s) is associated with meekness? How is this person(s) an example of meekness?

3. Do a concordance study of two synonyms of the word *meek*. How are these words used in the Scriptures, particularly in the New Testament? Does Matthew or the other Gospel writers employ *meek* or a derivative elsewhere?

4. Jesus attested to His own meekness in Matthew 11:28. What did He mean in that context? Give examples from the life of Christ of His meekness.

5. After studying the following references and others you may find helpful, write a definition using your own words for *meek*.

2 Corinthians 10:1ff

Galatians 5:22ff

Colossians 3:12

James 1:19-21

1 Peter 3:15ff

6. What has meekness to do with our self-estimation, interests in others, relationship with God? (See Phil. 2:1-11.)

7. Skim today's newspaper or a current periodical. What slogans, quips, or advertisements fly in the face of meekness?

8. The corresponding blessing for this beatitude is to inherit the earth. What does this mean for this present world and for our eternal future? (See Ps. 37:11; 2 Cor. 6:10.)

9. Do you believe that you as a Christian possess everything? How ought your life to look different in light of this discovery?

10. What life change must you make to pursue meekness? What three steps will you take this week to practice meekness?

For Further Study
1. Do a word study on inheritance and its relationship to the believer.
2. Memorize Matthew 5:5.

•TOOL CHEST•
(A Suggested Optional Resource)

THE SECRET OF HAPPINESS

The Secret of Happiness (Word Books) is Billy Graham's layman's commentary on the Beatitudes. Biblical happiness, he explains, can only be found in adopting and implementing the attitudes and values outlined in the Beatitudes. Each standard is defined and then applied to twentieth-century living. Obstacles are addressed, not ignored. *The Secret of Happiness* will inspire you to strive for a higher, holier lifestyle and to never vacillate from being a committed follower of the Lord Jesus Christ.

4

Blessed Are Those Who Hunger and Thirst for Righteousness

•FOOD FOR THOUGHT•

Jesus said, "Blessed are those who hunger and thirst for righteousness, for they will be filled" (Matt. 5:6). There are many sorts of hunger and thirst. There's the plain, ordinary desire for food and drink. Then there's what I call "people hunger." I remember, when my husband was traveling in his job for weeks on end, being hungry for him. Then when all our kids left for college, I would walk into their horribly tidy bedrooms and a terrible hunger that couldn't be satisfied would grip me. There is a hunger for knowledge, pleasure, or money too. But when Jesus said, "Blessed are those who hunger and thirst for righteousness, for they will be filled," He was talking about spiritual hunger and thirst.

The Bible talks much about being spiritually hungry and thirsty. On behalf of Jehovah, Isaiah invites all who are thirsty to come to the waters and all who are hungry to eat spiritual food that no money can buy. "Why spend money on what is not bread and your labor on what does not satisfy. Listen, listen to me, and eat what is good, and your soul will delight in the richest of fare" (Isa. 55:2-3).

The Apostle John issues a similar invitation to the thirsty in Revelation 22:17: "The Spirit and the bride say, 'Come!' And let him who hears say, 'Come!' Whoever is thirsty, let him come; and whoever wishes, let him take the free gift of the water of life."

Jesus Himself cried out in the temple courts on a great feast day, "If anyone is thirsty, let him come to Me and drink. Whoever believes in Me, as the Scripture has said, streams of living water will flow from within him" (John 7:37). Jesus promised He was the bread of heaven that could satisfy, and He was a well of life that could spring up inside and drench our souls with eternal delight! So we need to ask what is this righteousness that we will be blessed by pursuing?

John Stott in his book, *Christian Counter Culture*, says that there is legal, moral, and social righteousness. First of all, we must hunger and thirst after *legal* righteousness. We need to have a great desire to satisfy God's demands. God's righteousness is all that He demands and approves legally. God as my judge rightly condemns me for breaking His law. For me to have a religion that my soul hungers for, the Judge who has justly condemned me must, in grace and mercy, forgive me and waive my sentence. This He did at Calvary. The Pharisee in me objects—of course. Paul says the Jews, "did not know the righteousness that comes from God and sought to establish their own. They did not submit to God's righteousness. Christ is the end of the law so that there may be righteousness for everyone who believes" (Rom. 10:3-4). Self-righteousness won't save us—poverty of spirit will! Today people think that by going to church, being good, and trying to please God, they will win God's smile. But we can never be right enough to please His holy demands.

Second, there is a *moral* righteousness. This means developing our Christian character and conduct to match all that God demands and approves. Christ is our righteousness. We know God approves of Him! So we need to hunger and thirst to become like Christ. The Holy Spirit is given to us in order to produce this Christlike character within us. We cannot produce it ourselves.

Then there is *social* righteousness. It follows that as I hunger and thirst after righteousness, I will desire others do the same, that they too may enjoy this promised happiness. This will move me to loving action on their behalf and a lifetime of sacrificial service for a needy world.

In his book, *The Frog in the Kettle*, George Barna speaks of future trends saying: "Commitment is out. In the process of redefining what counts in life, many of us have decided that commitment is not in our best interests. Traditional concepts such as loyalty and the importance of membership in various groups have been thrown out in favor of personal interest and self-preservation. Commitment is viewed negatively because it limits our ability to feel independent and free, to experience new things, to change our minds on the spur of the moment and to focus upon self-gratification rather than helping others."[1]

If Jesus were living on earth in our 1990s, I doubt He would change

---

[1] George Barna, *The Frog in the Kettle* (Regal Books, 1990), pp. 33-34.

His message to meet the trends. Remember, the Pharisee in me seeks to load others up with heavy burdens, while the disciple in me seeks to bear other peoples' loads for them.

In Isaiah 50:4-5 the prophet describes God's perfect servant, the promised Messiah. He will have a great desire to teach the things His Heavenly Teacher teaches Him! The godly servant is ever conscious the teacher needs to be taught. Whereas the Pharisee is rebuked in Romans 2:21 with these words, "Thou therefore which teachest another, teachest thou not thyself," God's servant, in contrast, will hunger for truth early in the morning, tuning his ear to catch the many lessons he will need to pass on to others. Jesus said of Himself, "I do nothing on My own but speak just what the Father has taught Me" (John 8:28b). Through this self-discipline and commitment, the servant of the Lord will know how to console other hungry and thirsty people! If the prophet spoke like this about the Messiah, I, His humble disciple, can never think myself too big, too knowledgeable, or too qualified to pray! The Pharisee in me disagrees.

> "He tells me, 'Oh, you know enough
> just keep on with the same old stuff—
> you've books galore and tapes to lend,
> you've Christian magazines to send.
> No need to learn theology—'
> I've met the Pharisee in me!"

The Pharisee in me wishes to make it known that he thinks he is eminently qualified to teach others. What is more, he loves being recognized as a learned rabbi (Matt. 23:5). He is not adverse to being idolized either, even though Jesus had some strong words of rebuke for him. "Everything they do is done for men to see: they make their phylacteries wide and the tassels on their garments long; they love the place of honor at banquets and the most important seats in the synagogues; they love to be greeted in the marketplaces and to have men call them 'Rabbi' " (Matt. 23:5-7).

The Pharisee in me feeds on other people's approval, not on God's. It's hard to be satisfied with God's "well done" at the end of the day, but we must strive to make that goal our highest priority. So how do I practically develop a hunger and thirst for righteousness?

First, I'll need to recognize that the Pharisee in me will try to get me to be satisfied with lesser fare. He will prompt me to try to be a people pleaser instead of a God pleaser. We must not listen to him! We need to discipline ourselves to listen to God regularly, and not to listen exclusively to what others think of us.

Second, we should find or make faithful friends who will hold us accountable and not let us get too big for our boots. We need friends who will not be impressed with our so-called spirituality but who will accept us for who we are.

Third, if we know we love the chief seats in the synagogue (that's the Pharisee in us), we ought to deliberately abase ourselves and sit at the back!

Finally, we must check to see if we are spiritually alive! It is natural for a living person to be hungry. If we have no spiritual appetite at all, it may well be we have no spiritual life. If this is the case, remember Jesus said, "I have come that they may have life and have it to the full" (John 10:10).

Ask Him to give you eternal life—and you will be filled! Perhaps a simple prayer will help.

"Dear God, I have learned I cannot please You by good works. I understand Jesus, who always pleased You, can be mine and can give me His righteousness that You will accept. I ask Him to come into my life now. Lord, please forgive my sin of 'self-righteousness.' Fill my life by your sweet humble spirit, and help me to help others find Christ.   Amen."

Your name_____ Date_____

•TALKING IT OVER•

---

1. Review the definition of righteousness.
   Is it . . .

   □ your good works?   □ going to church?
   □ trying to please God?   □ being good?
   □ obeying the 10
      Commandments
   □ knowing Christ?

   Write a sentence explaining what righteousness is.

10 minutes

---

2. Read Isaiah 55.
   Discuss in groups:

   □ What do you learn about God?
   □ What do you learn about David?
   □ What do you learn about God's Word?
   □ What do you learn about the hungry and thirsty?
   □ What do you learn about yourself?

   Share with the large group one of the above.

20 minutes

---

3. Discuss the Pharisee in you.
   □ Where do you see him most clearly in your life?
   □ What's one step you can take to counteract his
      influence?

5 minutes

•PRAYING IT THROUGH•

Suggested Times

1. Praise Him for Christ who is our righteousness.	*3 minutes*
2. Pray for a hunger and thirst for His likeness in your life.	*3 minutes*
3. Pray for moral righteousness among... □ leaders and church members □ missionaries □ our children	*5 minutes*
4. Pray for social righteousness in our... □ neighborhood □ town or city □ country □ world	*5 minutes*
5. Pray for anyone in the group who isn't sure they have eternal life.	*4 minutes*

• DIGGING DEEPER •

1. What whets your appetite? What are you hungry for spiritually?

2. Recap Matthew 5:1-5, identifying who it is that is hungry and thirsty. Why do they desire righteousness and what do you think it means to the people you have described?

3. Does it surprise you that their desire is for righteousness? What things would you expect a Christian to be hungry for?

4. What is righteousness compared to in importance in 5:6? Is it so important to you?

5. A well-known Christian scholar once referred to this verse as a measure of one's Christianity (D. Martyn Lloyd-Jones, *Studies in the Sermon on the Mount*, pp. 74, 84, Eerdmans, 1979). If thirsting for righteousness is not fundamental to us, we should reexamine our commitment to Christ to ensure we are truly in Him. Take time to soberly reflect on your own spiritual condition.

6. Is the Lord Jesus primarily addressing a believing or nonbelieving audience? (cf. 5:1-12)

7. What does legal righteousness refer to? In light of the primary audience here, what kind of righteousness does Jesus most likely have in mind? (cf. 1 John 1:9; Matt. 6:1-2; Luke 1:6)

8. With a yearning for personal moral righteousness also comes a longing for social reform. What does the Bible teach about social

righteousness? (Lev. 19:15; Ps. 15; Micah 6:8) Can you give twentieth-century examples from church history and U.S. history of personal righteousness spilling over to a concern for social righteousness?

9. What is the unspoken blessing (the omitted object of the verb) that those who hunger and thirst for righteousness shall receive?

10. There is a perpetual pattern that occurs when we hunger and thirst after righteousness. Can you identify it?

11. Who satisfies our thirst? (cf. Ps. 107:9; John 4:17; 6:35; 7:37)

12. The paradox of Matthew 5:6 is that the more our desire for righteousness is satisfied, the more we shall long for absolute holiness (cf. 1 Thes. 4:7; 1 Tim. 4:7-8, 12, 15-16). When will our thirst for righteousness ultimately be quenched? (cf. Rev. 7:16-17)

Reflection
1. Are you pursuing blessedness or righteousness in your prayers?

2. Do you ache to be holy?

3. What is your greatest ambition?

4. What do you find the majority of your time and resources leave you pursuing (check your checkbook!)?

For Further Study
1. Read the article on righteousness in a Bible dictionary.
2. Consult D. Martyn Lloyd-Jones' notes on Matthew 5:6.
3. Memorize Matthew 5:6.

•TOOL CHEST•
(A Suggested Optional Resource)

STUDIES IN THE SERMON ON THE MOUNT
D. Martyn Lloyd-Jones' work on the Sermon on the Mount is considered a classic among evangelical theologians. Pointed, devotional, and practical, it speaks to the heart and mind of the reader. It is filled with quotable quotes you will want to remember for all kinds of life's occasions. This text is scholarly; yet, after reading each chapter the reader feels as if he has just sat under the teaching of a great preacher and Bible expositor, which he has.

5

Blessed Are the Merciful

•FOOD FOR THOUGHT•

"Blessed are the merciful," said Jesus, "for they will be shown mercy" (Matt. 5:7).

Richard Lenski says there is a difference between mercy and grace. "Mercy always deals with what we see of pain, misery, and distress which are the results of sin. Grace, on the other hand, deals with sin and guilt itself. Mercy extends relief while grace bestows pardon. Mercy cures, heals, and helps whereas grace cleanses and reinstates."[1]

Jesus invited a rich young ruler to show mercy in a very practical way. The young man was told to sell everything he had and to use the money to alleviate the needs of the poor. He turned his back on Christ's offer and went away sad. He didn't want to spend his money on mercy. Billy Graham paraphrases Matthew 5:7 this way, "They which have obtained mercy from God are so happy, they are merciful to others."[2]

God is a God of mercies. Paul says it's because of God's mercies we should present our bodies as living sacrifices (Romans 12:1). Nowhere is this principle seen as clearly as in the story Jesus told of the Good Samaritan. In the course of his daily life, a man was robbed and left for dead in a ditch. Other people passed by hurriedly, in case they too should be victimized. The Pharisee and the scribe hurried on to their church meetings, but a good Samaritan got down in the ditch with the man, poured oil and wine on his wounds, lifted him out, and took him to a place of safety. He then paid for the wounded man's care and promised to come back for him when he was well. We can see a

---

[1]John R.W. Stott, *Christian Counter-Culture* (IVP, 1978), p. 47.
[2]Billy Graham, *The Secret of Happiness* (Grason, 1955), p. 109.

beautiful picture of the Gospel in this simple parable (Luke 10:30-35).

Like the victim in the parable, we each go about our daily business when, unexpectedly, a thief robs us of our innocence, strips away our self-effort at godliness, and leaves us naked and helpless in God's eyes. Sin is that thief! We wait helplessly, our souls lying in life's ditch, while people pass us by—indifferent to our wounds and needs. We are half dead, and if Jesus doesn't come along, it will be too late and we'll soon be completely dead! Jesus, however, doesn't pass us by. Instead He reminds us of how much He cares. He gets into the ditch with us, puts His arms around us, and lifts us above our hurts. He paid for our healing with His own wounds. He was stripped naked and laid in His own ditch at Calvary for us. Isaiah tells us, "By His wounds we are healed" (Isa. 53:5). Like the Good Samaritan in Jesus' story, He promises to come back for us one day and take us home to heaven.

When I personally understand and respond to the mercy of God in Christ, then, overwhelmed with His grace and love, I will find myself healed. Christ's love for me will provide the motivation to set out from my inn, to climb down in the ditch with others—my family, my neighbors, my friends. My response to mercy must be to give mercy!

Mercy doesn't ask, "Does the man in the ditch deserve to suffer?" If mercy asked that, the answer would be yes! We all deserve to pay the price for our sin. Mercy, however, asks instead, "Does the man suffer?" If the answer is yes, then, because of His great compassion, mercy seeks to relieve the suffering one. Only God can show such mercy and forgiveness; only God can heal us from our past and give us a new life. Some of us are going to spend longer in the inn than others because some of us have more hurts that need mending than others. Some wounds may have been self-inflicted and some may have been inflicted on us, but God can heal us of them all. When the devil reminds us of our past, we need to remind him of his future and tell him our heavenly Good Samaritan has forgiven us, and he'd better get lost!

If you decide to be Christ's disciple and therefore live a Good Samaritan life, you will begin to resemble God. When you have compassion on souls that are half dead, you will be like him. Mercy is compassion in action. Jesus had compassion on the multitude because they were like sheep without a shepherd. Mercy acts. It isn't passive. It gets thoroughly involved in evangelism.

Next time you talk to unbelievers, try and have a mental picture of them lying in a ditch, half dead. Then realize you have the oil and wine that is needed to save them. You have the Christ. He is oil to soothe and heal, and wine to cleanse. He is life. What does a half-dead person—who will soon be wholly dead if someone doesn't help him—need? Life! He promises to give it to us more abundantly than we have ever had it before. Don't pass by other people's trouble and pain. Ask yourself instead, "Am I showing mercy by sharing my faith?"

But wait—there is a Pharisee in me. He thinks the whole idea is quite stupid. He's sure the silly man in the ditch deserves to be in his terrible predicament. "If he got himself into that mess he should get himself out," he says piously.

Shortly after returning from a third-world country, I was talking to a young businessman. He had little time for my stories of the poor and needy. "They should get a job. If you give them handouts, they'll stay in their ditch forever," he offered patronizingly.

"There are no jobs to be had," I replied.

"Then they deserve to be in the mess they are in," he rejoined. "Anyone can find work if they really want to. Anyway I've read about those people; they are lazy and don't produce."

"Maybe it's because they have to do any work they are lucky enough to find on half a cup of poor rice under the blazing sun," I told him. He wasn't interested. I was saddened at his attitude but began to wonder if mine was any better!

I recognized the Pharisee in me was prone to hurry by the man in the ditch, to get to my job at the temple! I'm secure, I thought. It's hard to understand someone out of work when you're employed, hungry when you're full, uneducated when you have college credits. It's so easy to fall into complacency and keep out of the sight of pain.

But there is a greater call even than the call to compassionately help people socially. There is the soul's need of a Savior. It's hard to remember what it's like without Christ when you've been a Christian a long time. The Pharisee can't remember because he's never experienced Christ's life. He's also quite forgotten any duty to relieve suffering along the way.

> "He passes people every day
> Who've lost their innocence some way.
> He says a prayer for that poor fool,
> for breaking his religious rule
> 'No time for mercy now,' says he,
> 'at Bible study I must be.' "

So we can have this pharisaical attitude toward those in dire straights spiritually as well as materially. "If they are lost, or in material need, it's their own fault," the Pharisee in me argues. "There are churches on every corner, and Christian TV and radio at the turn of a button. There are thousands of good Christian books that they could buy if they'd only spend their money on something worthwhile." What the Pharisee doesn't realize is that a lost man doesn't always have the will or the power to help himself to salvation. Often he's so wounded, we need to first show him mercy by loving practical acts. Then when he has benefited a little by our loving attention, he'll be able to listen to our message of salvation and respond. Acts of mercy open the door to sharing the Gospel. It was during my time in the hospital at the age of 18 that a girl showed me love, friendship, and practical attention—which I didn't deserve! Those acts of mercy opened my ears to hear about Christ the Good Samaritan, who eventually lifted me out of my ditch of despair.

Another name for mercy is forgiveness. You can't really talk about one without the other. If someone has forgiven us, we find it easier to forgive others. Meekness and mercy go together. The meek are also the merciful. The meek are willing to tell others that they are sinners too.

Another well-known story in the Bible tells us God is like a merciful Father ready to forgive us, thus releasing us to forgive others. Jesus told a story about two sons. One stayed home and one took off and squandered his life and living. He ended up in a ditch—or to be more precise, in a pigsty. Here, stripped of all but his life, "he came to himself" and figured out he was a fool to live in a pigsty when he could live in a palace. He decided to go home and throw himself on his father's mercy. This he did. He was lovingly received, forgiven, and restored to the previous privileged position he had forfeited for sinful pleasures (Luke 15:11-32).

Again the picture points out our desperate, willful plunge into independence and sin and God's willingness to forgive and restore us if we really are sorry! But there is a Pharisee in the story. Jesus paints a picture of an older brother. Proud and prigish, he despises his brother and hates his father for making a fool of himself by receiving the younger brother back home. He lashes out, accusing his father of being unfair. He refuses to rejoice at the return of the prodigal and ends up rejecting a loving offer of reconciliation.

> "He cannot see why he that sins
> when he's been careful of these things,
> should so receive the Father's smile

when he's been good for such awhile.
Why ring to do the Father's work
should he bestow on him that shirked?
Why shoes to show his kingly place,
Why robe to cover sin's disgrace?
So hate and animosity
spills from the Pharisee in me!"

The Pharisee in the story refused to rejoice in the forgiveness offered to the prodigal because he had never sought forgiveness himself. For the life of him he couldn't think of anything he needed to be forgiven for! Sitting in his pigsty of pride, he bitterly refused to forgive his brother. "It isn't fair," he burst out. "I've been so good and my father never gave me a party!"

The Pharisee is a prejudiced prig who may visit the church pew but never the altar rail. He prejudges people constantly, never bothering to get all the facts straight, and he is far too quick to condemn. Someone has said, "Being prejudiced is being down on what you're not up on!" The Pharisee will prejudge the father for receiving sinners in mercy. "This son of yours," he snaps. He despises his own birth relationship with his father and has no recourse for those who break or even bend his own rigid religious rules. The beam in his eye prevents him from seeing the mote in others' eyes and from seeing others as God sees them. Every time we are jealous when a sister or brother is "given a party" — that is, acknowledged in church, honored, or given credit — the Pharisee in me fumes with fury. "How could they pass me by?" we want to know.

Mercy is a Christian virtue developed by the disciple who would build his life on solid ground. Mercy breaks man's rigid, religious rules and obeys God's. When Jesus healed the blind man on the Sabbath, the Pharisees didn't ask, "Is the man healed?" and rejoice. Instead, they asked, "Who dared to heal him on the Sabbath?" Who had the right to break their rules, they wanted to know! Woe to us if we refuse to forgive, refuse to rejoice in the undeserving person who is converted to Christ, refuse to count him our brother, and refuse to seek our own prodigals in a loving, compassionate manner emulating our God. Mercy brings happiness home to our hearts, so let us build our lives on this firm footing. Then when the storms of judgment come, we will be shown mercy ourselves.

•TALKING IT OVER•

---

1. *Mercy Revealed*

    10 minutes

    ☐ Read Exodus 33:19. Why do you think this par-
    ticular revelation of God's character encouraged
    Moses at this particular moment?

    ☐ Read the whole of Nehemiah 9. What aspect of
    God's mercy touches you and why?

---

2. *Mercy Required*

    15 minutes

    Read Micah 6:8.

    ☐ Which part of this threefold requirement is the
    most convicting to you?

---

3. *Mercy Rejected*

    5 minutes

    Read the two verses about the elder brother in this
    chapter.

    ☐ Do you recognize the elder brother—
    the Pharisee in me?

    ☐ Discuss: how can we deal with him?

•PRAYING IT THROUGH•

Suggested Times

1. Praise God for His mercy.
   Meditate on Lamentations 3.
   Praise Him for all the things in these verses.

   10 minutes

2. Pray for God to work in unforgiving hearts.
   Ask Him to help you and others in this respect.

   5 minutes

3. Repent of pharisaism.
   Pray about getting involved in ministries of practical mercy such as . . .
   ☐ Salvation Army
   ☐ World Relief
   ☐ Your own church programs

   5 minutes

•DIGGING DEEPER•

1. What words are synonymous with or parallel to mercy in these verses and others you find on your own?

   Exodus 12:13

   Numbers 14:18

   Psalm 13:5

   Psalm 23:6

   Romans 12:1

   Colossians 3:12

2. Read Luke 18:10-14 and answer the following questions related to the Parable of the Pharisee and the Tax Collector.

3. Contrast the Pharisee's view of himself with the tax collector's view of himself. What did the Pharisee lack?

4. What was the tax collector's plea? How are mercy and humility related in this parable?

5. How are mercy and humility related in the Beatitudes? (cf. Matt. 5:5 and Matt. 5:7)

6. How are mercy and forgiveness related in the Parable of the Unmerciful Servant in Matthew 18:21-35? How are they related in the Beatitudes? (cf. 5:3-4 and 5:7)

7. How are you like the unmerciful servant? Think of a situation where you should have been more merciful. Confess it to the Lord and, if possible, make it right.

8. Who is it that is undeserving and in need of mercy in the Beatitudes? What is their attitude?

9. What do those who show mercy realize about themselves, and how does this prompt them to be more merciful?

10. Can we earn mercy by being merciful? If not, what is the underlying principle here? How can we show we are truly sorry for our sins? (Matt. 5:3)

11. Would those who know you well describe you as a merciful person?

12. Who do you know who is needy, miserable, or guilty in your congregation, office, or neighborhood? How could you show them compassion?

13. See your local newspaper. Who in your community is in distress, and how can you help?

For Further Study
1. Read two chapters of your choice from John Stott's *Involvement: Being a Responsible Christian in a Non-Christian Society.*
2. Memorize Matthew 5:7.

•TOOL CHEST•
(A Suggested Optional Resource)

INVOLVEMENT: BEING A RESPONSIBLE CHRISTIAN IN A NON-CHRISTIAN SOCIETY

Mercy is at an ebb in our non-Christian society. Christians who shy away from personal involvement in the world's staggering social dilemmas are perhaps as guilty in their omission as those inflicting the oppression. What can I do? What difference could I make? These are soul-searching questions, but inadequate excuses for declining to participate in the often slow and painstaking solution process.

Volume I of *Involvement* is John Stott's heroic answer to such questions and practical exhortation to encourage Christians to good works and appropriate social action. He exposes evils in areas such as politics, human rights, economics, and environmental concerns and shows how Christ's love can be demonstrated in each. Stott gives historic precedent for Christian involvement in most stratas of society and evidence of the changes wrought by just such involvement. This book will spur you on to mercifully bringing the whole Gospel to the whole world without prejudice and assist you in finding your place in ministry in the field of social concerns.

6

Blessed Are the Pure in Heart

•FOOD FOR THOUGHT•

Jesus said if you are looking for happiness, make sure you have a pure heart (see Matt. 5:8). "That doesn't sound like too much fun," a teenager responded when I made this startling statement in a youth meeting. The devil would have us believe that to be pure is to be puritanical in the very worst sense.

The Greek word for *pure* means unadulterated, that is, not mixed with anything foreign. It can be used of milk that has not been watered down. It can also be used to describe clothes that have been thoroughly scrubbed or dishes that have been well washed. Webster defines the word *pure* as "free from foulness or dirt from guilt or the defilement of sin. Innocence, chastity; free from any sinister or improper motive or views."

To be pure involves purity of heart and mind and soul. It speaks of sexual purity—in the workplace and in all our relationships. The world and the devil laugh out loud and throw the word *Victorian* at those who would be pure of heart or at anyone talking about chastity today.

"Who wants to be chaste?" people inquire. "That's so old-fashioned." And we can be hard put to answer when we know that most teens have usually had their first sexual experience by the age of sixteen. Surveys taken across Christian college campuses indicate that most sexually active young people don't believe there is anything wrong with believers indulging in sex outside of marriage.

How is it our young people have rewritten the rules so readily? Is it because we each have an impure heart that wants to rewrite God's rules? The Bible says that after the Fall man's "heart was only evil continually" (Gen. 6:5, KJV). God knows this to be the truth because He can see deep down inside us (1 Sam. 16:7). In case we were left with any false ideas, Jesus Christ told us that out of a man's heart come "evil thoughts, murder, adultery, sexual immorality, theft, false testimony, and slander" (Matt. 15:19). What is more, a heart like this will not be inclined to reform or change. Each person needs a transplant—a new heart, a new nature—if he or she is to desire to live a life free from inner impurities, whose natural end is outer sinful actions.

When we are born again, God gives us His own pure heart. Now, "born again" does not mean "start again." If the old heart or old nature or the flesh as the Bible calls it, tries to start again and live a pure life, it will certainly fail. We need a whole new heart in order to succeed. We need a new spirit of willingness to do the things necessary to live a holy life which is truly pleasing to God.

Now the Pharisee in me doesn't like all this talk. He believes his old heart is perfectly capable of pleasing God. Why, he is so pleased with its religious efforts, he cannot imagine God being any less thrilled! So he polishes up the outside of his life, leaving the inside dirty. Jesus called this *hypocrisy* (Matt. 23:25-26). He described the Pharisees as whitewashed tombs—looking clean outside while inside they were full of dirt and death. We cannot hang religion all over the outside of our lives and expect God to be pleased. If we work from the outside in instead of the inside out, we will not be accepted by a holy God.

> "He laughs when told of a pure heart,
> And wants no parcel or no part
> of looking in and seeing sin
> when such a perfect man he's been.
> He spends his life in holy work
> and never quits and never shirks.
> He shines the outside of his cup,
> and knows not that he'll finish up
> in dungeon deep, in hell's abyss—
> cause God condemns a man like this!"

The problem is—even after I have received my new heart, the old heart is still there! As I begin to look after my "new" nature and keep myself pure, the old heart or nature fights me every inch of the way! The Pharisee in me won't sing the sort of hymns that contain such sentiments as:

"Throw light inside the darkened cells
where passion reigns within;
quicken my conscience till it feels
the loathsomeness of sin."
(*Keswick Hymn Book*)

So how do we ignore the Pharisee's protests and keep our hearts pure? David has the answer for us in Psalm 119:9-11.

How can a young man keep his way pure?
By living according to Your Word.
I seek You with all my heart;
do not let me stray from Your commands.
I have hidden Your Word in my heart
that I might not sin against You.

"Your Word," David also said, "is a lamp to my feet and a light for my path" (Ps. 119:105). As the light of His Word pierces the darkest recesses of our hearts and the innermost core of our beings, it will expose every corner, leaving each of us with a daily choice. We can die to the dirt—repent and ask God to clean the inside of our cup—or ignore—yea, rather chloroform our conscience—and join the world. How does this work in practical terms?

Perhaps you are a teenager and you have been invited to a somewhat exciting, yet risqué, party. I remember that happening to me shortly after being converted to Christ. "Flee youthful lusts" (2 Tim. 2:22, KJV), said my Bible. "Remove thy foot from evil" (Prov. 4:27, KJV), and "your body is the temple of the Holy Spirit" (1 Cor. 6:19). I was being reminded to live according to His Word, so I didn't go to the party! That's how it works. And how do we hide God's Word in our hearts? We do that by reading it, memorizing it, and obeying it. This way we will not sin against God.

But what happens if we can't do what we are supposed to do, and we blow it? What happens then? Well, this very same David who gives us such wonderful advice and inspires us to heed God's precepts and obey His laws, lost his own purity one day. It happened like this. It was spring and he was 50 years old—a heady combination. It was time for war, but David stayed home and sent Joab, his military commander, instead. In essence he said, "Here am I—send Joab!" David was lazy and stayed in bed until evening. Add his laziness to Bathsheba's loneliness (her husband was away fighting), and you get the picture. Satan saw a golden opportunity and made sure Bathsheba took her bath in full view of the king. The rest is history. David committed adultery, had Bathsheba's husband killed in battle, and settled down to enjoy the fruits of his labor. In a master understatement, 2 Samuel 11:27 says, "The thing David had done displeased the Lord."

One year later God spoke to David through Nathan the prophet and called him to account. David responded at once. "I have sinned," he acknowledged. Terrible repercussions followed. He had already lost his purity and his friend; now he lost his child, and the respect of Joab, whom he implicated in Uriah's murder. Most of all David lost his precious relationship with God! Out of his guilt and shame the man who wrote Psalm 42:1, "As the hart pants after the waterbrook, so my heart pants after You, Oh my God," now penned Psalm 51.

If we look at this psalm we can get some help for our own times of defeat. The first thing to do is to respond to God's word of rebuke, however it comes to us. It may come through the Bible, a preacher, book, tape, or just through the still, small voice of conscience. We need to confess we have sinned (Ps. 51:3), and then we need to ask God to cleanse us and make our hearts clean again. Next, we should realize that any sin against man is a sin against God (v. 4). Remember, He expects us to be open and honest with Him about it all (vv. 5-6). We need to let God renew our spiritual relationship with Him (vv. 7-11). He is the only one who can create a pure heart in us again. Once the Lord has forgiven us, we should ask Him to restore the joy of our salvation, renew our evangelistic zeal, and sustain a willingness to nurture a broken and contrite attitude in order not to repeat the offense (vv. 12-17).

One day Jesus stopped a mob from stoning a woman who had been taken by the Pharisees from the bed of her lover. She was an adulteress. The Pharisees wanted Jesus to condemn the woman, but He told them, "If any one of you is without sin, let him be the first to throw a stone at her" (John 8:7). One by one, from the oldest (and wisest) to the youngest hothead, they left! The outside of the Pharisees' lives might have looked as if they were sexually pure, but they knew perfectly well that the inside was full of dirt.

Never say never. Any one of us can fall. But a life lived close to Christ and lent His power to be obedient to His Word, will be focused on God and rewarded with His smile!

"Blessed are the pure in heart for they shall see God."

•TALKING IT OVER•

1. Share an experience of a spiritual *heart transplant,* a conversion experience, either yours or someone else's (e.g., John Newton who wrote the hymn "Amazing Grace" after he was saved, and who had been a notorious slave trader).

   8 minutes

2. Read Psalm 51 and match the verses to the words:

   ☐ Respond ☐ Request ☐ Realize ☐ Regret
   ☐ Receive ☐ Renew ☐ Restore

   7 minutes

3. (Group discussion)
   ☐ What does the world say about purity?
   ☐ What does God say?
   Read the following verses:
   ☐ 1 Peter 1:16
   ☐ Hebrews 12:14
   ☐ Psalm 24:3-4
   ☐ 1 Timothy 5:22
   Restate them in your own words.

   15 minutes

•PRAYING IT THROUGH•

*Suggested
Times*

1. (On your own) Praise God for giving us Christ's heart. — *2 minutes*

2. (On your own) Repent of impurity. (Be specific.) — *3 minutes*

3. (Together) Pray for those who need a Psalm 51 experience (no names). — *5 minutes*

4. Choose a verse from Psalm 51 that encourages you and tell why. Thank God for the verse. — *5 minutes*

5. Pray for: — *5 minutes*
   ☐ ministers of the Word—that they would faithfully teach it
   ☐ listeners of the Word—that they would faithfully obey it
   ☐ all of us—that we may hide His Word in our hearts that we might not sin against Him.
   Memorize Psalm 119:9-11.

•DIGGING DEEPER•

1. Let's examine the meaning of *pure in heart.* What is the word *heart* parallel to in these two references?

   Deuteronomy 6:5

   Jonah 2:3

   What is its meaning in Matthew 12:40?

2. In Proverbs 4:23 heart is synonymous with "wellspring of life." What does this expression mean?

3. Besides meaning the center of man's life which rules his physical, mental, and emotional personality, what else does the biblical definition of heart refer to in 1 Samuel 16:7?

4. What is the natural condition of man's heart according to the following verses?

   Genesis 6:5

   Jeremiah 17:9

   Matthew 15:19

   Romans 1:21

   Romans 2:5

5. Is there a biblical solution? (cf. Jer. 24:7; Ezek. 11:19; Eph. 3:17)

6. How does a person receive this pure, undivided, unadulterated heart?

Psalm 51:1-4

Psalm 51:10, 17

Ezekiel 18:31

Jeremiah 31:33

Ephesians 3:17

How may a Christian keep his or her heart unadulterated?

Psalm 119:9-16

Proverbs 4:20-22

Proverbs 4:23

Matthew 5:3

Matthew 5:4

Acts 13:22

8. Identify the scriptural incentives for keeping the heart pure.

Hebrews 12:14

1 John 3:2-3

9. Who may see God; that is, who will be accepted before God?

Psalm 24:3-4

Psalm 51:6

Psalm 73:1

Acts 15:8-9

10. What kind of purity does the context of the entire Sermon on the Mount promote as opposed to the purity the Pharisees proposed?

11. In what common situations does inner impurity often take place, and how can it be recognized?

12. What concerns do you face today (a broken relationship, new home, death of a loved one, career change, new phase in a child's life, etc.)? Describe what a pure heart would look like in each situation.

13. How is to "see God" fulfilled both in this present life and in our eternal state?

14. Make a chart for each day of this week, charting the number of times you catch yourself daydreaming or "vegging out" and tell where you find your thoughts dwelling each time. Do you notice any impurities (i.e., are you in agreement, supporting or implementing anything insincere, immoral, false, deceitful, hypocritical, etc.)?

Days of the week, number of times daydreaming, and about what:

Mon.	Tues.	Wed.	Thurs.	Fri.	Sat.	Sun.	

For Further Study
1. Memorize a verse that was meaningful to you in this study.
2. Memorize Matthew 5:8.

•TOOL CHEST•
(A Suggested Optional Resource)

LOVING GOD

Pure in heart. How does one become so? Charles Colson's section titles from *Loving God* (Zondervan) give us a clue: Obedience, the Word of God, Sin and Repentance, The Hunger for Holiness, The Holy Nation, Loving God. What holds you back from wholeheartedly, single-mindedly pursuing a pure heart? If you are a risk-taker, dare to delve into *Loving God* and allow the Spirit of God to confront your hidden agendas, habits of the heart, and secret sins. Give Him the opportunity to eradicate them from your heart, mind, and body. Without this eradication we will not see God exalted in eternity, nor recognize His plans and purposes in this life. Colson has a rare gift for cutting to the heart of things. Let him cut out those things in your heart that are impure and keep you from becoming all God would have you to be.

7

Blessed Are the Peacemakers

•FOOD FOR THOUGHT•

In his book, *The Secret of Happiness*, Billy Graham says, "Jesus didn't leave a material inheritance to His disciples. All He had when He died was a robe, which went to the Roman soldiers; His mother, whom He turned over to His brother John; His body, which He gave to Joseph of Arimathea; and His spirit, which returned to His Father. But Jesus willed His followers something more valuable than gold, more enduring than vast land holdings, and more to be desired than palaces of marble—He willed us His peace. He said: 'My peace I give unto you: not as the world giveth, give I unto you. Let not your heart be troubled, neither let it be afraid' " (John 14:27, KJV).[1]

The world will certainly have plenty of toil and trouble to offer us, so how are we going to cope with the conflict? Will we respond with worry and fear, or with peace of mind? Jesus is the Prince of Peace. The problem is, people are looking for peace without the Prince. Some might even claim to have found tranquility, but God's Word says if they do claim to have found peace, it is only a temporary or false peace if it discounts the Prince! Some search for peace in possessions, others in alcohol, and still others in a secure relationship. But the simple fact of the matter is, there can be no real peace in the world until we have peace with God.

Someone has said in the last 4,000 years there has been a scant 300 years of real peace. One cannot help but wonder whether, even in that 300 years, that small amount of peace has been universal. Ever since man rebelled—declaring war against the Almighty and in so doing

---

[1]Billy Graham, *The Secret of Happiness* (Grason, 1955), p. 168.

following Satan's example—there has been an enmity between God and man. Christ, however, came to earth to bring reconciliation and peace. Didn't the angels sing "peace on earth to men on whom His favor rests"? (Luke 2:14) When Christ died on the cross, He made that peace possible (Col. 1:20; Rom. 5:1). Now we can receive His spirit of peace in our hearts. He is our peace, says Paul (Eph. 2:14).

"The tranquility of order" that St. Augustine spoke about can become ours. Our circumstances may be pretty stormy, but as we build our lives on the Rock, Jesus gives us His peace. This peace "transcends all understanding" (Phil. 4:7). It "garrisons" our hearts and minds—that is, it puts a guard around us so the troubled thoughts that would besiege us are kept at bay! In other words, there can be peace within while there is war without. In fact, in Psalm 27, David exults, "Though war break out against me, even then will I be confident" (v. 3b). We must be very careful to realize this peace we are speaking about is not "peace at any price." In fact, it was procured at an enormous price. It cost Jesus, God's Son, His life.

It follows quite naturally that the disciples of Jesus should model themselves after their Prince. He is the peace giver—they are the peacemakers. This sort of service follows naturally out of an experience of Christian conversion. But He warned it will take pain to produce peace between people. There will be the pain of apologizing, the pain of being misunderstood, the pain of offering an act of mercy which may well be thrown back in our faces. However, we must persist if we would be like our Master.

Not only will this process be painful and require patience, but we will need power that will be quite beyond our own human resources. Being selfishly oriented we won't want to bother getting involved. We'll give up on seemingly impossible situations and tell ourselves the price we have to pay is unnecessary and uncalled for! It is just as well Jesus didn't react to our dilemma in such a fashion. He Himself will equip us by His powerful Holy Spirit.

So where are these peace efforts to take place? First and foremost in our marriages. If you are unmarried, be very careful to choose a Christian partner. If you marry outside of Christ, you will find yourself and your spouse on opposite sides of the fence. That is asking for trouble. If you are a woman and have found Christ since you married, read Proverbs, Chapter 31. Realize you need to make your husband happy, and let God make him good! If you are fortunate enough to be married to a godly man, there will still be ample cause to play the peacemaker. This is nothing to do with "appeasement" but rather practicing a loving, giving, sacrificial lifestyle that models Christ's peaceful, loving attitude to His bride—the church.

Another place we can get busy being a peacemaker is within the family itself. If we have children, there will be no lack of opportunity to tell the kids it's time to visit "Camp David" when hostilities break out. I heard about a very busy businessman who traveled a lot, but who promised his son that if he ever really needed him, he was to call and the father would come home. One day, on the evening of a big business venture in another city, the boy called and said, "Dad, I need you; please come home." The father came, packed up his son, and went off to "Camp David." He took time out—not without cost—to help his boy make peace with God, with his father, and with his world. He was a wise man who loved the Prince of Peace and was committed to being His agent in this world.

When siblings "get at" each other we can referee by making sure they "fight clean." Sometimes subtle diplomacy will be needed. An egg timer helps to give the warring factions equal time to state their cases and ensure both parties listen. Make sure as arbitrator that both parties are "hearing" what is really being said. So often trouble arises because what is being "heard" is not what is being said! Sometimes it helps to write to an offended one rather than talk to him or her.

The third area in which we need to function as peacemakers is in the church. Paul wrote to a "fellow yokefellow" to help two strong women he loved and admired—his companions in the faith—who had come to spiritual blows! Their names were Euodia and Syntyche.(My husband nicknames them Odious and Soon Touchy! Know any women like that?) Anyway, Paul plays peacemaker by writing a letter and appealing to a third party to help these ladies resolve their differences. Possibly this true "yokefellow" turned into scrambled eggs by the time he was finished, but I'm sure he tried anyway! We must do the same. Peace after all is "made"; it doesn't just happen.

Now the Pharisee in me hates the very thought of all this. Far from being a peacemaker, he is a peace breaker, a veritable warmonger. He is like the elder brother in the story of the prodigal son (Luke 15:11-32). When his father appeals to him to do the right thing and forgive his brother, he refuses to even face him. He pouts and complains that no one ever gave him a party, so he's not about to give his good-for-nothing brother a party. After all, the brat doesn't deserve it. And even though . . .

"The father reasons with the son
that mercy and forgiveness won . . .
the offending brother be restored
that retribution be outlawed,
that loving welcome be extended,
instead, the Pharisee's offended.
He wants the boy to crawl, you see,
I've met the Pharisee in me!"

But isn't this what "mercy" is all about? Extending forgiveness to people who don't deserve it one little bit? Of course it is! Those of us who build these Christian principles into our lives will find its own reward. For didn't our Prince of Peace, Jesus, tell us, "Blessed are the peacemakers for they will be called sons of God" (Matt. 5:9). Like the Father, like the Son you see.

Let us, therefore, go about our Father's business bearing His likeness!

•TALKING IT OVER•

1. (Group discussion) Read John 14:27.
   What does this verse say about:
   □ God?
   □ The world?
   □ Us?

   10 minutes

2. (In pairs) Read Colossians 1:20.
   Discuss how you would explain this verse to someone who had never heard of Christianity.

   10 minutes

3. It takes—
   Pain ⎫
   Patience ⎬ to produce peace
   Power ⎭

   10 minutes

   Which of these have you experienced as you
   have tried to effect peace in some relationship?
   Share your answers.

• PRAYING IT THROUGH •

Suggested Times

---

1. Praise the Lord for the Cross and the price He paid to effect peace with God for us.

5 minutes

---

2. Pray for peace to come in
   □ marriages
   □ families
   □ communities
   □ the U.S.A.
   □ the Middle East
   □ the world

5 minutes

---

3. Pray for the peacemakers:
   □ in the world
   □ in the church
   If appropriate share a prayer need in this regard.

5 minutes

---

4. Pray for yourself with a partner.

5 minutes

•DIGGING DEEPER•

1. Take a moment and brainstorm a list of various kinds of peace.

2. How is the word *peace* defined in the dictionary? Does a Bible dictionary contribute anything more to your understanding of the word?

3. Jesus is our finest model of a peacemaker. What peace did He provide, how did He do it, and who did it affect? (cf. Rom. 5:1; Eph. 2:11-22; Col. 1:20)

4. Review the Beatitudes. What peace is foremost in Matthew 5:9?

5. If we have received peace with God, how ought we to be primarily involved in peacemaking? (cf. Rom. 10:14-17; 2 Cor. 5:18-20)

6. What other kinds of peacemaking ought we to practice as a result of the Gospel's work in our lives? (cf. Rom. 12:18; 1 Cor. 7:15; Heb. 12:14; 1 Peter 3:11)

7. According to the verses in exercise 6, what is the Christian to avoid?

8. How can we put this principle into practice?

Matthew 5:44-45

Luke 17:3

James 1:19-20

Other verses:

9. To be God's son is to share in His character or likeness. If we become peacemakers, how shall we be like our Heavenly Father? What shall be our reward?

10. How does 1 Peter 3:8-12 restate the Beatitudes?

11. Is there someone with whom you need to be sharing Christ? Seek the Lord for wisdom, words, and the opportunity to do so.

12. Is there a relationship in your life that needs mending? What would Christ have you say or do to heal it?

13. Are there two parties at discord in your life? Are you in a position to reconcile them? Commit each to prayer and ask for guidance to know how you could help bring them back together.

For Further Study
1. Read *In the Gap* by David Bryant.
2. Memorize Matthew 5:9.

•TOOL CHEST•
(A Suggested Optional Resource)

IN THE GAP

"Blessed are the peacemakers." Blessed are those who stand in the gap available to be used as tools to help men be reconciled to God. The gap is as wide as eternity, for sin is its measure. In this book David Bryant's powerful challenge calls Christians and churches to examine their roles as peacemakers. Bryant will help you see the reality of this world without Christ. He answers the questions, "What does it mean to be a world Christian?" and "How can I have a global influence for the Gospel?" Two of the appendixes in this tool will help you utilize it more effectively. The first is a ten-week, small-group study guide complete with questions for using *In the Gap*. The second is a personal strategy guide for applying the principles found within. There is also a resource list of books, periodicals, and organizations to assist you in your study. Allow *In the Gap* to help you conform to Matthew 5:9.

8

Blessed Are Those Who Are Persecuted

•FOOD FOR THOUGHT•

Whenever I allow myself to think of the subject of persecution, I treat it a bit like a terminal illness. "Oh, it will never happen to me," I assure myself. As I have been forced to face Matthew 5:10-12, I have come to the conclusion I need to start saying "when" it happens, not "if" this should ever happen. In John 15:18-26, we read that Jesus left His disciples in no doubt as to what they could expect. "If the world hates you," the Lord warned, "remember that it hated Me first." He went on to explain that a servant is not greater than his master and "if people persecuted Me—they will persecute you too." "The world" here refers to the human system that opposes God's purposes.

Paul takes up the theme in his letter to suffering Christians, reiterating "all that will live godly in Christ Jesus shall suffer persecution" (2 Tim. 3:12, KJV). He didn't say "may suffer" or "may not suffer"— he said "shall suffer." The Lord, however, promised that "happy are they who are persecuted for righteousness' sake" (Matt. 5:10, KJV). There will be a special blessing for those who are subjected to such honorable trouble. Note we receive His blessings when we are persecuted "for His sake." There will be no such help and happiness for those who suffer because of their own stupidity! As Peter himself warns us in 1 Peter 4:12, the reason for the hostility generated against disciples of Christ, is that evil hates goodness, darkness hates light, lies hate truth. We will be persecuted for the "Word's" sake, we are told—Matthew 13:21 and Mark 4:17.

This persecution will take various forms ranging from being railed upon or yelled at, to being socially ostracized or separated from people's company—all the way to being separated from our breath! In fact, Jesus said it would not be uncommon that "anyone who kills you will think he is offering a service to God" (John 16:2)

So what joy could we possibly find in being murdered for our faith? What did Jesus mean when He said we should jump up and down for joy if we were abused on His behalf? (Matt. 5:12) Part of the joy will be the realization that we are part of a great heritage. "Rejoice and be exceeding glad," said Jesus, "for so persecuted they the prophets which were before you" (Matt. 5:12, KJV). The prophets, being salt, arrested the corruption that was in their world. They found their message unacceptable to the world system presided over by Satan who happens to be "prince of this world" (John 12:31).

Jeremiah was cruelly treated; Zechariah stoned to death for declaring the truth (2 Chron. 24:20-22); and Isaiah, according to Jewish tradition, was sawed in two inside a log by wicked King Manasseh! This is tough stuff, yet it is a reason for pride in the privilege of following in the train of martyrs. If we take on Satan's system, we can be sure the Satan of the system will personally take us on.

We must not be too surprised if some of this persecution is dressed up in religious garb. It certainly was in Jesus' case. Stephen died because he accused the overly religious Jews of murdering the Messiah (Acts 7:52).

The persecution that began to be perpetrated against the first Christian believers stemmed from the fanatical Jewish leaders. The second persecution that arose came from the Romans—for their own religious reasons. They accused the Christians of cannibalism (stemming from misinterpreting the practices of Communion) and homosexuality (being wrongly deduced from their "love feasts"). The religious Romans accused the Christians of atheism—i.e., refusing to acknowledge or believe in the Greek and Roman gods.

What is called "the great persecution" began when Rome very nearly burned to the ground during the great fire of Rome. Suspicion fell on the Emperor Nero, whereupon he deflected it by claiming the Christians set the city alight. He followed his accusations up with terrible torture; Christians were burned, and killed by gladiators and wild beasts. Many died in the great arena in Rome and in other cities too.

Polycarp, Perpetua, and Blandina were three of the most famous martyrs to suffer and die at this time. But what a triumphant parade they made of it all, going to their deaths with joy and singing, counting it all joy to be so identified with their Savior in His death.

Having warned of persecution in this life, Jesus made it clear that there was a line the persecutors could never cross. That line was death. "Great is your reward in heaven," He assured His followers (Matt. 5:12). The early Christians expected suffering. They believed there was no greater honor than to imitate the death of Christ through accepting martyrdom. Christian witness by one's blood, they believed, meant Christ would actually be present with them in some mystical way, and they testified to the fact of that experience with their dying words.

Ignatius of Antioch said—
"Near to the sword,
I am near to God;
In the company of wild beasts,
I am in company with God.
Only let all that happens be in the
name of Jesus Christ,
so that we may suffer with Him.
I can endure all things if He enables me."

while Papylus of Thyateira prayed—
"Blessed are You, Lord Jesus Christ,
Son of God,
for You have, in Your mercy,
been so kind
as to allow me a death like Yours."[1]

So when I think of "when" and not "if" I am to suffer persecution, I remind myself of something else. When I catch myself in some "small trouble" and hear the petulant Pharisee in me objecting to such cruel usage by saying "why me?"—I try to tell him that, for the Christian, suffering is inevitable. I just need to look around and think of all the people who have it a whole lot worse than I do. It has been said there have been more martyrs at the end of the 20th century than in the entire history of the Christian church. If that is so, when the Pharisee in me says "why me," I can answer him—"why not!"

Jesus told us that not only was suffering inevitable for His followers, but that it was also a test of true discipleship. He told a parable of the sower going out to sow his seed. Some fell on stony ground where it took root but did not go deep enough. When the sun came up, it withered (Matt. 13:6). Jesus said that the sun is a picture of persecution. When the heat is on a plant which is shallow and superfi-

---

[1]Dwayne W.H. Arnold, *Prayers of the Martyrs* (Zondervan, 1991), pp. 58, 78.

cial, it shrivels up. Those folk who make sure God's words fall deeply into their souls will stand firm when testing comes.

All this sounds pretty scary, doesn't it? In the light of many who are paying for their faith with their lives in other parts of the world, we realize those of us who live in the West enjoy comparative freedom to practice our beliefs. Perhaps persecution comes in more subtle ways for us. Maybe our reputation is martyred, our feelings crucified, or our motives slaughtered. Perhaps we will not be included in a party, or our children may be shunned by other children. Whatever form persecution takes, the Lord promises to give power and grace to stand it.

When Corrie ten Boom was a little girl she worried aloud to her father about not denying her Lord should she ever be tortured for her faith. He told her not to worry. "When you get on the school bus, I give you the penny for the fare," he said. "God, your Heavenly Father, will do the same." We cannot imagine how we could ever be brave enough to witness for Jesus in the face of such terrible persecution as Corrie endured but, like her, we do not need the courage now. If (or when) it happens, He will empower us as we need. In other words, Jesus is waiting at the bus stop. He will actually get on the bus with us, pay the fare, and accompany us to our destination, however terrible.

So take courage. We should expect that if we kick the devil, he will kick us right back, but we must also remember the devil is like a vicious animal. God may permit Satan some leeway for His own purposes, but He firmly holds the end of the leash! Persecution comes only by divine permission.

When Shadrach, Meshach, and Abednego were thrown into the fiery furnace, the watchers were astonished to see not three men but four—walking around in the intense heat (Dan. 3:25). One, we are told by the eyewitnesses, looked like "a son of God." God delivered the three men "in" the fire as well as "out" of the fire, and we must believe He will do the same for us. Paul put it well—he reminded us that "our light and momentary troubles are achieving for us an eternal glory" (2 Cor. 4:17).

When we think of Paul's "light and momentary" troubles as he describes them, we realize our own little troubles are absolutely nothing in comparison. However, he is trying to remind us that there are special honors awaiting those who suffer for righteousness' sake, and we need to encourage ourselves with such heavenly promises.

So rejoice if you are counted worthy to suffer for His sake—for so persecuted they the prophets before you—and remember, "great is your reward in heaven!" (Matt. 5:12)

"The Pharisee reviles the one
who tries to follow God's dear son.
He persecutes the witness who
confesses Christ his whole life through.
He murders life when e'er he finds
disciples who with peace of mind,
refuse to cower or bow the knee,
to him—the Pharisee in me.

I know the Lord rebukes my guest
in scathing words, at God's behest.
He tells me "heed his words of strife
and realize he saps your life."
He hates to share my heart, you see,
with him, the Pharisee in me.

And why should He the God of grace
be forced to live here face to face
with him who hung Him up to die.
against an angry anguished sky—
who pierced His feet and crowned His head,
who laughed, and left Him very dead?
Forgive me, Lord, I beg of Thee,
deal with the Pharisee in me!"

•TALKING IT OVER•

Suggested
Times

1. (On your own) Look up the following verses and
   write a personal thought by each reference (one
   sentence).
   Persecution was predicted by Jesus . . .
   ☐ Matthew 16:21
   ☐ Matthew 17:22-23
   ☐ Mark 8:31
   He said it was a test of true discipleship . . .
   ☐ Mark 4:17
   and a means of blessing . . .
   ☐ Matthew 5:10-11, and 12
   He warned of its severity . . .
   ☐ John 16:2
   ☐ Matthew 23:34
   but promised there was a line beyond which perse-
   cutions were unable to go . . .
   ☐ Matthew 10:28
   ☐ Luke 12:4
   (In group discussion) Share your thoughts from this
   study out loud.

   25 minutes

2. Read the whole *The Pharisee In Me* poem. Discuss
   which verse meant most to you and why.

   5 minutes

•PRAYING IT THROUGH•

Suggested Times

1. Praise God for the way Jesus bore persecution for us in order to procure our salvation.   *5 minutes*

2. Pray for people TODAY who are suffering persecution.   *10 minutes*
   - ☐ those in prison for Christ's sake
   - ☐ missionaries
   - ☐ Christians in the marketplace
   - ☐ Christians in marriages or families hostile to their profession of faith
   - ☐ Christian children in secular schools and colleges

3. Share a persecution you or someone close to you is enduring (first names only). Pray for those people. Pray for strength, courage, and joy "when" your time comes.   *5 minutes*

•DIGGING DEEPER•

1. How is the blessing in this Beatitude qualified? (Matt. 5:10)

2. How are the subjects of verses 9 and 10 connected in this passage? (Matt. 5:3-10)

3. What are the prerequisites for entrance into the kingdom of heaven in Matthew 5:3 and 10?

4. What kind of persecution did Jesus predict? (cf. Matt. 16:21; John 15:18-20; John 16:2)

5. On what principle did He base His prediction? (cf. John 15:18-20)

6. Look up these biblical examples of suffering persecutions for righteousness' sake. What do they share in common?

    Acts 4:1-22   Peter and John

    Acts 5:17-40   The Apostles

    Acts 7:54-60   Stephen

    Acts 16:16-40   Paul and Silas

1 Peter 4:12-19   Believers

7. What does persecution include in Jesus' expansion of the idea? (cf. Matt. 5:11-12) Can you give examples from His own life of enduring such persecution?

8. What is "because of righteousness" in Matthew 5:10 parallel to in verse 11? What righteousness is in mind then?

9. State the command in verses 10-12. Identify the motivation for obedience to this command.

10. What is the biblical perspective Christians are to have on suffering?

    Matthew 5:12

    2 Corinthians 4:17

    1 Peter 1:6

    1 Peter 3:13-18

    1 Peter 4:13

    1 Peter 5:10

11. Whose example is to be an encouragement to us? (cf. Matt. 5:12) Can you recall specific people from the Bible or tradition who could encourage you in times of difficulty?

12. What is persecution a sign of?

13. How do the values in the Beatitudes set the believer apart from the secular world in which he or she lives? (cf. John 17:14-18)

14. Review all eight chapters. Which Beatitudes do you need to incorporate into your own life? Prioritize your list. Now make a personal plan of attack for adapting each one. Include prayer and action steps.

For Further Study
 1. Read the Christian classic, *Fox's Book of Martyrs.*
 2. Memorize Matthew 5:10-12.

•TOOL CHEST•
(A Suggested Optional Resource)

WHERE IS GOD WHEN IT HURTS?
When we suffer for the sake of righteousness, we may, like Job, be tempted to ask, "Where is God when it hurts?" Phillip Yancey understands our questioning. In *Where Is God When It Hurts?* (Zondervan) he discusses all manner of suffering. The author divides his work into three parts:

Part 1: Why Is There Such a Thing As Pain?
Part 2: How People Respond to Extreme Pain.
Part 3: How Can We Cope with Pain?

Yancey's book is more than theological. It is deeply personal. He personalizes pain by including numerous accounts and conversations from saints who are suffering and whose lives are ridden with pain. Yancey shows the reader the difference it makes to be a Christian when suffering.